For Carrie and Nick

Published in 1989 by Warwick Press,
387 Park Avenue South, New York, New York 10016.
First published in 1989 by Kingfisher Books Ltd.

Copyright © 1989 by Grisewood & Dempsey Ltd.
All rights reserved
5 4 3 2 1

Library of Congress Catalog Card No. 89-50003
ISBN 0-531-19067-6

Printed in Italy

I like Music

BARRIE CARSON TURNER

WARWICK PRESS

Contents

Introducing Music

Music was important to the first people who lived on Earth. Their music was not the music we know today. They banged sticks and stones together to make loud noises, and blew through reeds and shells to make whistling sounds. They sometimes used their music to frighten off prowling animals, and sometimes, as we do, to express happiness and celebration as well as sadness.

Today, music is still as important to us, whether we dance to it, sing to it, or just listen to it. Many people play a musical instrument as a hobby and enjoy going to concerts. We hear music on television, at the movies, and even in supermarkets as we do our shopping. Music is everywhere!

This book will tell you about instruments in the orchestra and in pop music, and how to make instruments of your own. It looks at how music affects our lives, and suggests some ideas for making up your own music. You will find out how to read music and learn to play simple tunes on the recorder or piano, and to accompany yourself, or a friend, on the guitar. So turn the page and start reading about, and making, music. Have fun!

All Kinds of Music

For hundreds of years music has been written and played in many different ways and for many different occasions. At an opera or at the ballet, the audience sit quietly in their seats, listening and watching. At a pop concert the audience joins in with the performance — thumping out the beat and singing along with the music.

How many different kinds of music can you think of? Look at these two pages and you will see examples of all kinds of music.

▲ Chinese opera is a mixture of dance and singing.

◀ A jazz band in New Orleans.

▲ Folk singers in Puerto de la Cruz, Tenerife.

▼ The clog dance from the ballet *La Fille Mal Gardée*.

▼ Bob Marley sings reggae.

▲ This orchestra is making a recording in a studio.

◀ A flute player in the State Police Band in Bahrain.

▲ The Phantom sings in Andrew Lloyd Webber's musical *The Phantom of the Opera*.

◀ A brass band in the Swiss Alps.

▼ *Dire Straits* in concert.

▼ A band playing at a carnival in Brazil.

Instruments Around the World

Musical instruments are found in all parts of the world — many countries have their own special instruments. Look at the map and you will see some instruments that you will recognize and some unusual ones.

Some instruments have not changed for hundreds of years and are still played in the traditional way — the Scottish bagpipes, for example. Others have been invented more recently. The West Indian steel drums, which make a beautiful ringing sound, are made from old oil drums. Have you ever seen any of the instruments in the pictures?

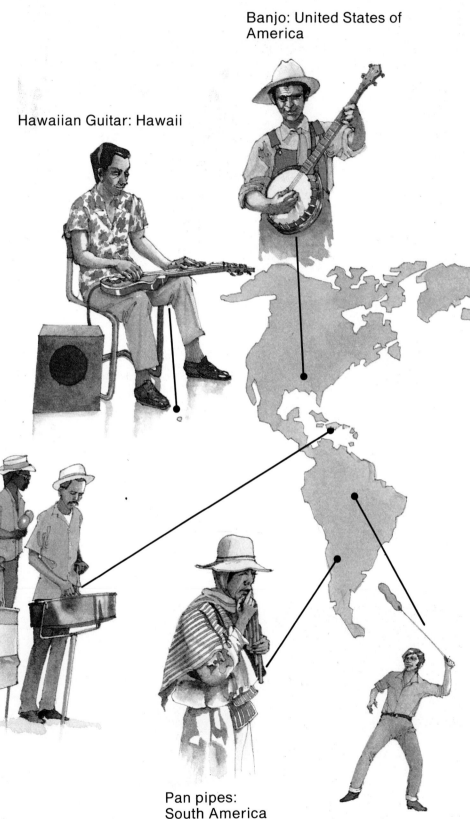

Banjo: United States of America

Hawaiian Guitar: Hawaii

Steel drums: West Indies

Pan pipes: South America

Bullroarer: South America

Scottish bagpipes: Scotland

Mandoline: Italy

Cimbalom: Hungary

Balalaika: Soviet Union

Koto: Japan

Gamelan orchestra: Indonesia

Drums: Africa

Sitar: India

Didgeridoo: Australia

11

Long and Short Sounds

In the world around us some sounds are **LONG**.

And some sounds are SHORT.

When you read and play music you need to know how **LONG** or SHORT each sound is.

Note shapes

When music is written down, each sound or note has a special shape. The different note shapes tell you how long or short the musical sounds will be. Here are some note shapes and their names:

𝅝	Whole note (semibreve)
𝅗𝅥	Half note (minim)
𝅘𝅥	Quarter note (crotchet)

Playing at a steady speed

Always try to play your music at a steady speed. For the music on these two pages, try counting a steady 1-2-3-4 before you start, and during the music. Each note shape is worth a different number of counts:

𝅝	A whole note (semibreve) lasts for 4 counts. **1** 2 3 4
𝅗𝅥	A half note (minim) lasts for 2 counts. **1** 2 3 4
𝅘𝅥	A quarter note (crotchet) lasts for 1 count. **1** 2 3 4

Clapping note shapes

A group of note shapes which you clap or tap is called a **rhythm** (*ri-thum*). Try clapping these rhythms — remember always to count a steady 1-2-3-4 before you begin. Keep counting as you clap. Only clap once for each note shape.

Whole note rhythm

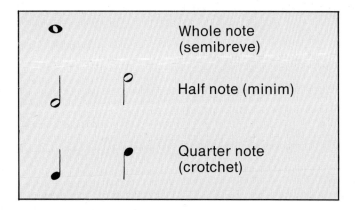

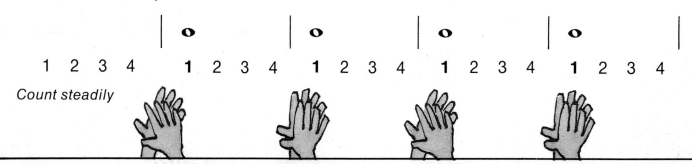

1 2 3 4   **1** 2 3 4   **1** 2 3 4   **1** 2 3 4   **1** 2 3 4

Count steadily

Half note rhythm

Half notes last for two counts each, so clap on counts **1** and **3**.

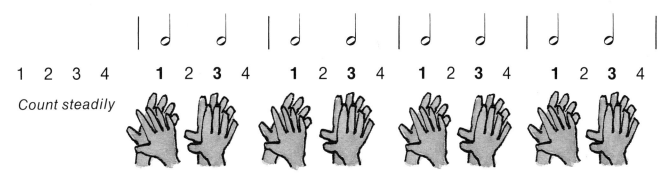

Quarter note rhythm

Quarter notes last for only one count each, so clap on counts **1,2,3** and **4**.

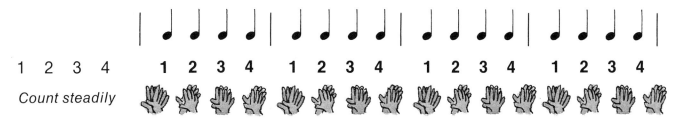

Mixed note rhythm

The lines that divide up the groups of notes are called **bar lines**. The music between each bar line is called a **bar**. Different length notes can be mixed up in one bar — but if you are counting 1-2-3-4 for each bar the notes must always add up to 4 counts. Watch carefully for the changes of note.

Dividing up a whole note into shorter notes is like sharing your chocolate chip cookie. Break it into two and you have two halves, break it into quarters and you have four quarters.

High and Low Sounds

In the world around us some sounds are HIGH. And some sounds are LOW.

When you read and play music you need to know how HIGH or LOW each sound is.

The stave

The note shapes are written on a set of five lines called the **stave**.

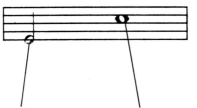

Notes are written with the line going through them . . .

. . . as well as in the spaces between the lines.

Some instruments play only high notes and others play only low notes, so most music is written on two different staves.

Music for high instruments or voices is written on the **treble clef** stave.

Music for low instruments or voices is written on the **bass clef** stave.

Reading high and low notes

A stave is like a ladder. How high or low the musical sound is depends on where on the stave the note shape is written. The higher up the stave a note is, the higher the sound will be.

This quarter note is lower down the ladder and will sound lower than the note above it.

This half note is higher up the ladder and will sound higher than the note below it.

When notes are higher than the middle line of the stave their stems point down.

The names of the lines and spaces

The lines and spaces of each stave are named after the first seven letters of the alphabet — **A,B,C,D,E,F,G**. As the notes move up the stave the letters move up the alphabet. The bottom lines of the treble and bass staves start at different places in the alphabet. At **G** the musical alphabet starts again. The silly sentences will help you to remember the names of the lines and spaces.

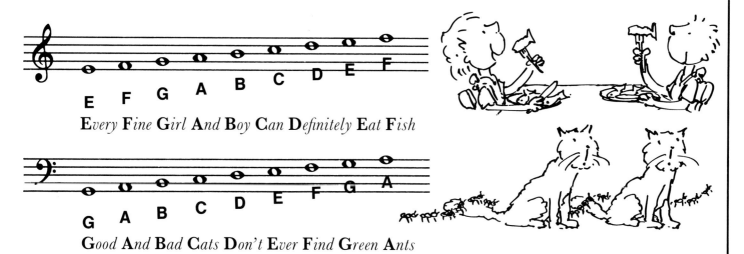

Every Fine Girl And Boy Can Definitely Eat Fish

Good And Bad Cats Don't Ever Find Green Ants

Fitting the note shapes into the lines and spaces

Here is your first piece of real music! It is the mixed note rhythm that you clapped on page 13. The rhythm is now a tune, because the note shapes tell you how long or short each note is, and how high or low it is. You could sing this tune or play it on an instrument.

There are lots of other things to learn about reading music, but now you know the names of the notes and how long or short they are, you could try some of the recorder and piano tunes later in the book, or you could strum some chords on the guitar as an accompaniment for a friend.

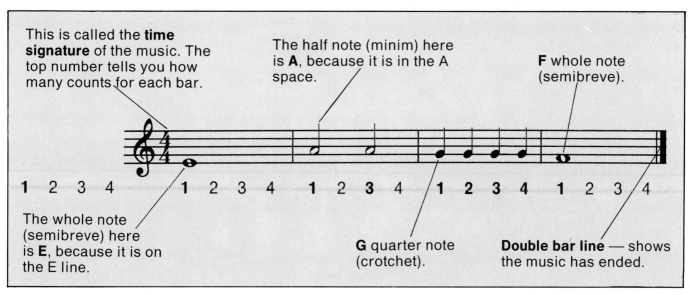

This is called the **time signature** of the music. The top number tells you how many counts for each bar.

The half note (minim) here is **A**, because it is in the A space.

F whole note (semibreve).

The whole note (semibreve) here is **E**, because it is on the E line.

G quarter note (crotchet).

Double bar line — shows the music has ended.

About the Orchestra

An orchestra is a large group of instruments, all playing together. The instruments of the orchestra can be divided into four sections. See if you can find these four different groups in the picture below.

Strings: instruments played with a bow — an arched stick with hair stretched across it.

Woodwind: instruments made of wood or metal. The player blows into or across the mouthpiece to produce a sound.

Brass: instruments made of metal. They are played by pressing the lip into the mouthpiece and blowing.

Percussion: instruments that are hit or shaken to produce a sound.

The Conductor

The person standing in front of the orchestra is called the **conductor**. He or she beats time or "conducts" the orchestra, showing the players how fast the music should go, as well as other things such as how loud or soft they should play.

Can you Conduct?

This is how the conductor indicates 2, 3, and 4 counts or "beats" in a bar. Use your right hand and follow the direction of the arrows.

The short stick which the conductor holds is called a baton. It helps the players to see the conductor's beat. When you are practicing your conducting try using a pencil as a baton.

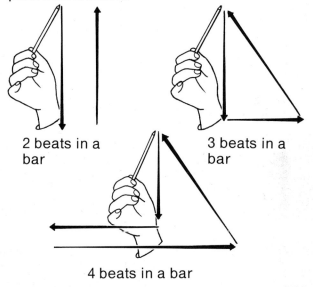

2 beats in a bar

3 beats in a bar

4 beats in a bar

Can you find these instruments in the picture of the orchestra on the opposite page? Which section of the orchestra do they belong to? (Turn to page 44 for the answers.)

◀ Double basses

◀ The harp

▲ Bass clarinet and bassoons

▲ The violin

◀ The cymbal, xylophone, bass drum, and gongs

▲ Trombones

Activity

The Recorder

There are many different sizes of recorder. The Sopranino is a small instrument which plays very high notes. The Great Bass is a large instrument which plays low notes. The three recorders that you are most likely to meet are the Descant, Treble, and Tenor, but it is the Descant recorder that you will be learning about here.

Descant   Treble   Tenor

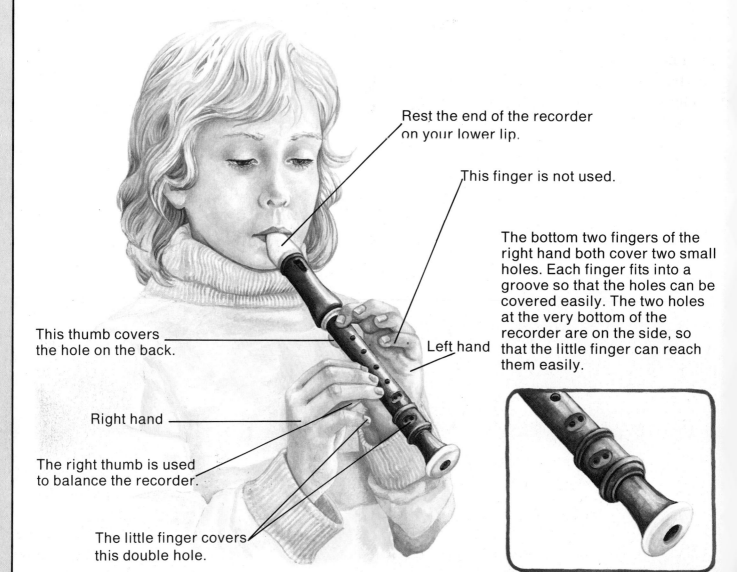

Rest the end of the recorder on your lower lip.

This finger is not used.

The bottom two fingers of the right hand both cover two small holes. Each finger fits into a groove so that the holes can be covered easily. The two holes at the very bottom of the recorder are on the side, so that the little finger can reach them easily.

This thumb covers the hole on the back.

Left hand

Right hand

The right thumb is used to balance the recorder.

The little finger covers this double hole.

Playing the Recorder

Rest the recorder on your lower lip and hold it so that you are not covering any holes. Blow gently and listen to the sound.

Now blow very hard. What happens to the sound? When you are playing the recorder, try to blow evenly. If you blow too gently the sound will be shaky, if you blow too hard it will be harsh.

When you blow a note on your recorder try whispering "too" or "doo." This is called tonguing and it helps you to produce a clean start to the beginning of each note.

Your first notes

The Descant recorder plays high notes, so music for it is written on the treble clef.

Here are some notes for you to play. Look carefully at the illustrations to see which fingers should cover which holes. Make sure that your fingers cover the holes completely, but there is no need to press too hard.

Practice box

Play these notes down, up, across or any way you like!

B	G	E	D
A	D	B	A
B	E	G	B
A	G	D	E

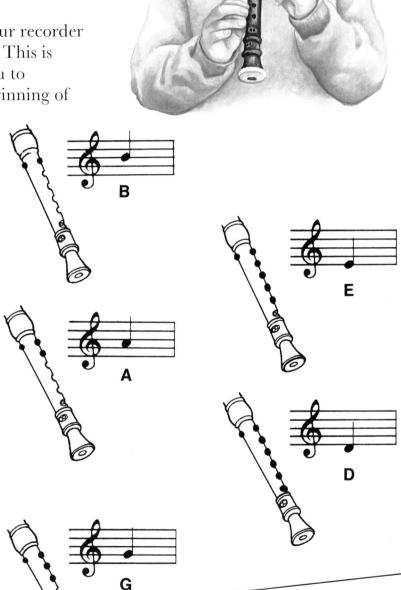

Important!
Try to change between notes quickly and smoothly. If the notes you are playing squeak or wobble it means that either you are not covering the holes properly, or you are blowing too hard. Practice slowly at first — then try speeding up.

Recorder Tunes

These tunes use the notes that you learned on page 19. Play them slowly at first, until you get used to the fingerings. Good luck!

Folk Tune

Gently

Breathe when you see this sign.

Westminster Chimes

Slowly

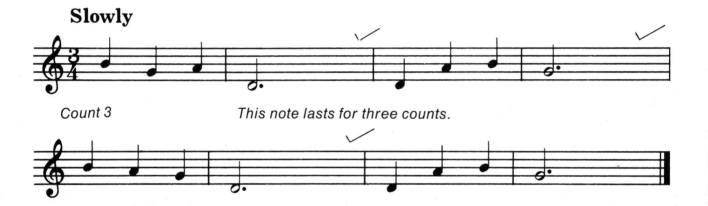

Count 3   *This note lasts for three counts.*

Three more notes

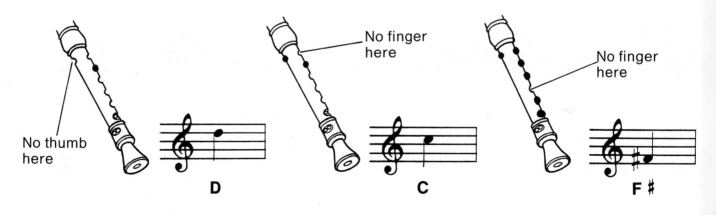

No finger here

No finger here

No thumb here

D   **C**   **F ♯**

Practise the three new notes that you learned on page 20 and then try
playing *Oranges and Lemons* and *Good King Wenceslas*.

Oranges and Lemons

Not fast

Good King Wenceslas

Brightly

Instruments of the Orchestra 1

Violin

The violin is the smallest member of the strings section of the orchestra.

Violin

Double Bass

The double bass is the largest string instrument in the orchestra. It has a very deep sound. To play it the player usually sits on a high stool. String players (especially double bass players) often pluck the strings with their fingers, instead of using the bow. This is called **pizzicato**.

Double Bass

Cello

The full name of this instrument is the violoncello, but this is usually shortened to cello. It is held between the player's knees, and supported by a metal **spike**.

Cello

—Spike

Viola

Viola

The viola is slightly larger than the violin and makes a deeper sound. It is played in exactly the same way as the violin. The sound of all these string instruments is made bigger, or **amplified**, by their hollow wooden bodies.

Clarinet

Keys

Clarinet

The clarinet is not only used in orchestral music but also in wind bands and jazz groups. It has **keys** which the player presses to open and close the holes.

Bassoon

Mouthpiece

Flute

The first flutes were made from bone, ivory, or wood, but modern flutes are usually made of metal. The flute can play very high notes. To play the flute the player blows sideways across the **mouthpiece**.

Crook

Flute

Bassoon

The bassoon is related to the oboe but plays much lower notes. The tube of the bassoon is almost ten feet long — so long that it has to be bent back on itself. The mouthpiece is at the end of a curving metal tube called the **crook**.

Reed

Oboe

The name of this instrument comes from the French word "hautbois," meaning "high wood" (the oboe is made of wood and can play high notes). The sound of the oboe is made by blowing through two thin pieces of cane, called a **reed**.

Oboe

Instruments of the Orchestra 2

Trumpet

Trumpet players produce different notes by changing the pressure of their lips, as well as opening and closing the three **valves**.

Valves

Trumpet

Trombone

The trombone player uses a **slide** to produce different notes. This is a section of tubing inside another tube which can be pulled out or in, and can make the tube of the instrument longer by over three feet.

Tuba

The tuba plays the lowest notes of all the brass family. The **mouthpiece** of the tuba is very wide and covers most of the player's lips. Although the sound of the instrument is thick and heavy it can still play lively music quite easily.

Tuba

Mouthpiece

Horn

The horn (sometimes called the French horn) is a very old member of the brass family. The tube or **bore** of the horn is very narrow and almost 13 feet long. The horn is played with the player's hand inside the **bell** at the end of the instrument.

Horn

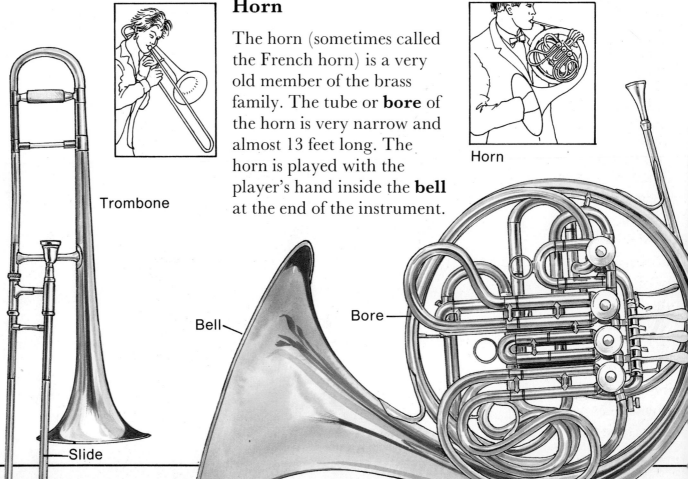

Trombone

Bell

Bore

Slide

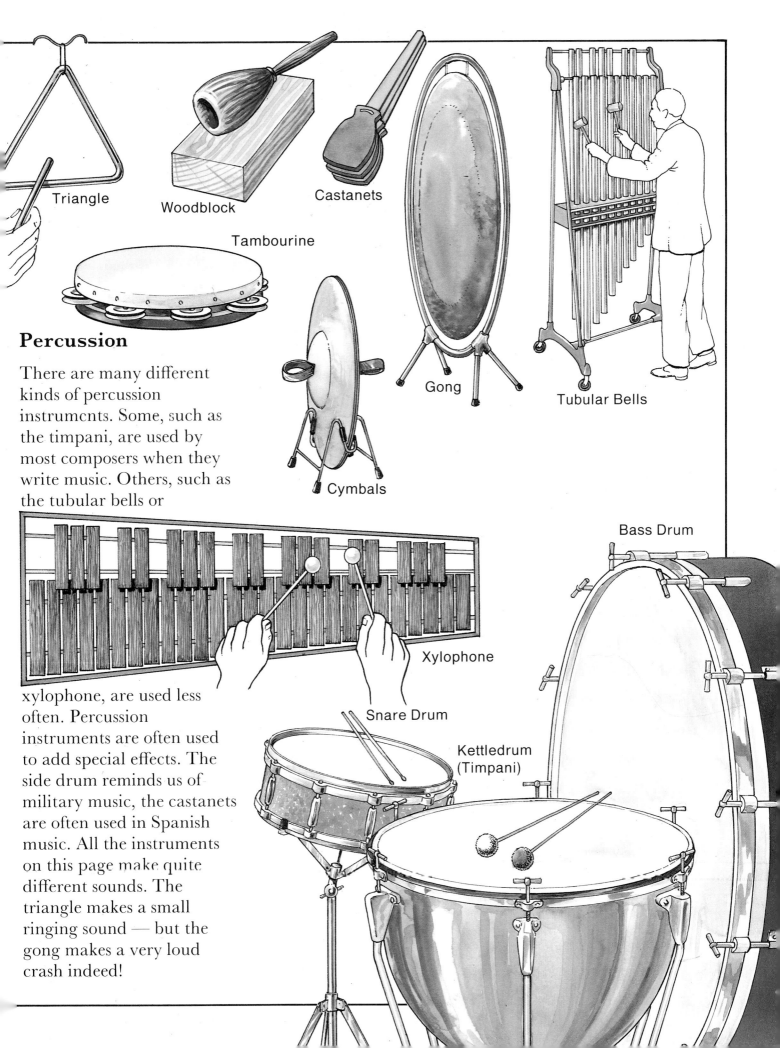

Triangle

Woodblock

Castanets

Tambourine

Gong

Tubular Bells

Percussion

There are many different kinds of percussion instruments. Some, such as the timpani, are used by most composers when they write music. Others, such as the tubular bells or

Cymbals

xylophone, are used less often. Percussion instruments are often used to add special effects. The side drum reminds us of military music, the castanets are often used in Spanish music. All the instruments on this page make quite different sounds. The triangle makes a small ringing sound — but the gong makes a very loud crash indeed!

Xylophone

Bass Drum

Snare Drum

Kettledrum (Timpani)

The Piano

Pianos are made in many different shapes and sizes, but the one you are most likely to see is the upright piano. It is called this because the strings stand up in the case of the instrument. You will probably have seen another where the strings lie flat. This is the grand piano. This instrument needs more space and is usually only used for special occasions, such as concerts.

Have a look at a piano at school or at home and see if you can find all these different parts:

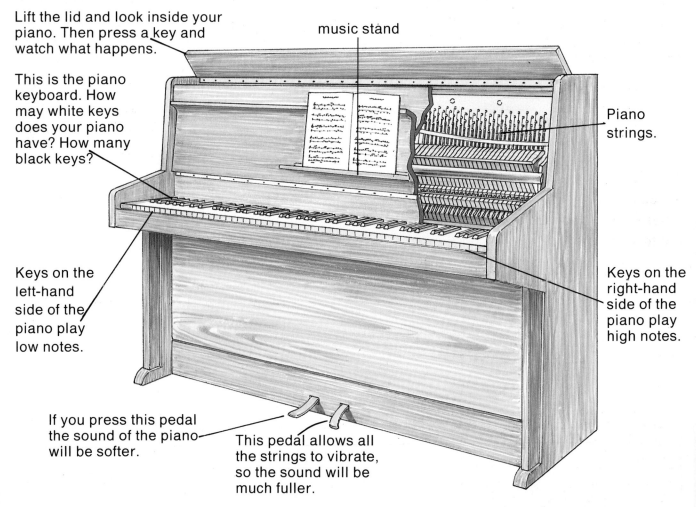

Lift the lid and look inside your piano. Then press a key and watch what happens.

This is the piano keyboard. How may white keys does your piano have? How many black keys?

Keys on the left-hand side of the piano play low notes.

music stand

Piano strings.

Keys on the right-hand side of the piano play high notes.

If you press this pedal the sound of the piano will be softer.

This pedal allows all the strings to vibrate, so the sound will be much fuller.

Inside your Piano

When you press a key down on your piano, two things happen at once. The damper pulls away from the string, and the hammer hits the string, striking the note that you hear. As soon as you release the key the damper goes back onto the string, stops it vibrating, and the note stops.

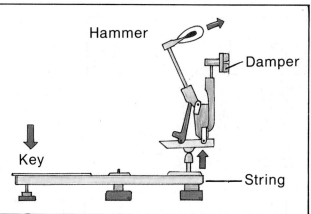

Hammer

Damper

Key

String

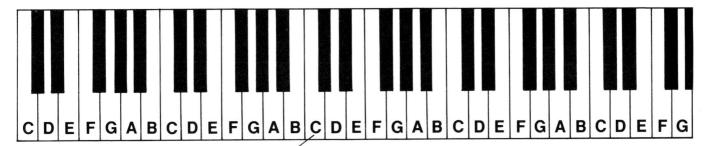

Every D on the piano comes between a group of two black keys.

This **C** is called **middle C** because it is near the middle of the piano.

G and **A** are between every group of three black keys.

Every **C** on the piano comes just before two black keys.

You can try all these exercises on an electric keyboard as well as on a piano.

The black keys on the piano form a pattern. The keys are in twos and threes. The pattern of the black keys will help you to remember which note is which. Play the notes **C**, **D**, **G**, and **A** on your piano. Now try to find the notes **E**, **F**, and **B**.

Practice Box

Find and play these notes. Read the box up, down, across or any way you like:

A	C	B	G
F	D	E	F
C	B	D	A
A	E	G	C

Finger numbers

When you play the piano, the music will tell you which fingers to use. It is important to use the correct fingers because this will help you to play the music smoothly. Here are your finger numbers:

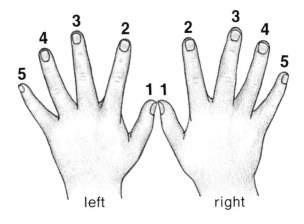

left   right

Now place both thumbs (finger 1) on **middle C** and spread your fingers out:

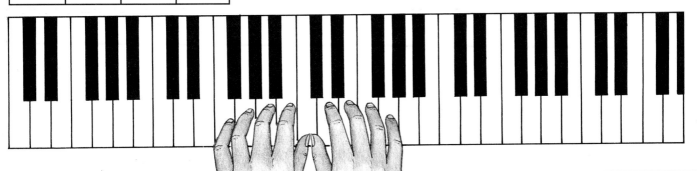

Piano Tunes

The piano plays high and low notes, so piano music is written on both the treble and bass clefs.

Place both thumbs (finger 1) on **middle C** and spread your fingers out, one for each key. Play the notes **F,G,A,B,C** with your left hand, and **C,D,E,F,G** with your right hand. These are the notes you will be using to play the tunes on these pages. Play the notes slowly at first.

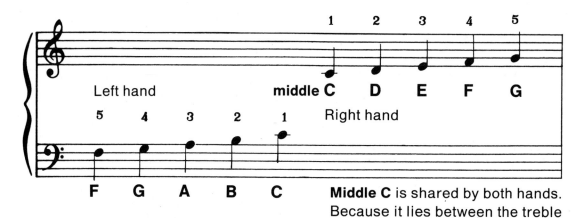

Middle C is shared by both hands. Because it lies between the treble and bass staves it is given a little line of its own.

Climbing Tune

Slowly

White Sand and Gray Sand

Moderately

Sitting at the Piano

When you are playing the piano, make sure that you are sitting on a stool or hard chair which is the right height for you.

Your back should be straight.

You should be able to reach the keys easily without stretching.

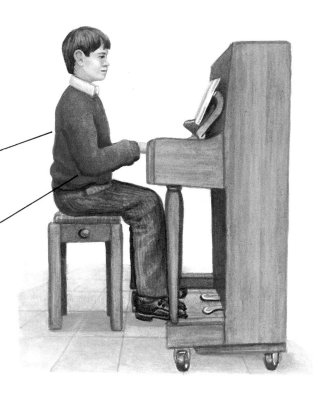

Indian Drums

Rhythmically

Instruments in Pop Music

All sorts of different instruments are used in pop music, but the instruments you will see most often are the guitar, bass guitar, drums and cymbals, and keyboards. "Keyboards" can include anything from a grand piano, like the one above, to the most up-to-date synthesizer.

Most of the instruments used in pop music are "electric" instruments which have to be plugged into an **amplifier** in order to produce any sound. Sometimes the musicians in a band play more unusual instruments: do you recognize any of the instruments in the pictures below?

▲ The marimba is like the xylophone (*see page 25*), but it has metal tubes called resonators underneath which improve the sound.

▲ Two kettledrums (timpani) and a gong make up part of the unusual percussion section in this band.

On the keyboards the player can produce the sounds of many different orchestral instruments as well as the piano and organ, and many more unusual ones.

▲ You will occasionally see wind instruments, such as this saxophone, in a band. The saxophone is related to the clarinet.

▲ Many different-sized drums and cymbals make up the drum kit.

► Guitarists often sing as well as play. The bass guitar (*on the left*) has only four strings, and plays lower notes than an ordinary guitar.

Making your own Instruments

You can make musical instruments out of all sorts of things. Some things can be played just as they are — such as stone clappers. Other things can be made into musical instruments quite easily. If you want to decorate your instruments you will find some ideas on page 35.

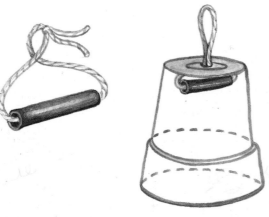

Make a spool beater with an empty thread spool and a piece of garden cane. Ask an adult to help you if the end of the cane needs filing to fit the spool.

You can use the spool beater to play your clay pot bell.

Clay Pot Bells

You can make bells out of clay plant pots.
1. Thread a piece of rubber tubing onto some string and tie the ends of the string together.
2. Thread the string through the hole in the bottom of the pot.

Bottle and Jar Chimes

Find some old, empty jars and bottles and tap them with your spool beater. If you stand them on a hard surface you will get the best sound. Now try filling them with different levels of water. What happens to the sound?

Rhythm Sticks

For tapping out rhythms all you need is two pieces of thick garden cane.

Stone Clappers

Two pieces of smooth stone make good clappers. Make sure you don't catch your fingers in the middle!

Wood and Metal Blocks

Use any small wooden box, or empty metal can to make these instruments.

Coconut Clappers

You will need two hollow coconut shells to make these clappers. Ask an adult to make a hole in the top of each one. Thread through a piece of string with a large knot in it. You can play this instrument by clapping the two halves together, or by tapping one half like a bell.

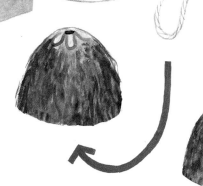

More Instruments to Make

Coat Hanger Chimes

You will need a coat hanger, some strong thread and a mixture of long and short nails to make this instrument.
Use the nails with the best "ring." Pick the best nails, arrange them in order of size, then tie a loop around the head of each nail and attach them to the coat hanger.

Stick Scraper

Thick garden cane with notches cut into it makes a good scraper. Ask an adult to help you to cut the notches.

Sandpaper Blocks

Find two blocks of fairly thick wood and pin sandpaper around the wood with thumbtacks. Rub the blocks together to make a scraping noise.

Cheese Grater Scraper

Find an old cheese grater and a wooden spoon. Rub the spoon against the grater for a good scraping sound.

Nail Beater

Tap a nail very gently into the soft middle part of a garden cane. You can use your nail beater to play the Coat Hanger Chimes.

Jingle Stick

You will need 24 pieces of aluminum foil, a garden cane, and four paper clips. Open out the paper clips, leaving a hook in one end, and thread six aluminum disks onto each clip. Bend the other end of the clips around a notch in the cane.

Box and Brush

Use an old washing powder packet and a shoe brush for this instrument. To play the Box and Brush hold the box between your knees and brush away from you.

Shakers

Collect different-sized plastic or cardboard food cartons and fill them with dried peas, rice, nails, or sand. Seal the tops with a lid or some aluminum foil.

Tambourine

Glue three paper plates together and attach jingles around the outside to make a tambourine. You might need an adult to help you push the paper clips through the cardboard. Leave one part of the edge free of jingles so that you can hold it.

Decorating your Instruments

When you have made your instruments why not decorate them? You can use felt tips, paint, crayons, decorated sticky tape, and food coloring to dye the water in your Bottles and Jar Chimes.

Garden Label Clackers

Tie four or five plastic labels together with a wire tie. Hold them firmly in one hand and flick them with the other, or on the edge of a table to make a buzzing sound.

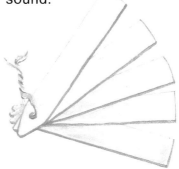

The Guitar

The guitar is one of the most popular instruments today. You will see it on television and hear it on the radio, and of course most pop groups and bands have at least one guitarist. If you follow the instructions here you will soon be able to accompany your own singing, or a friend playing another instrument.

When you play the guitar it is best to sit on an upright chair that has no arms. Cross your legs and rest the guitar on your leg. Your left hand will need to be free to move around, so make sure that it is not supporting the guitar. Try not to tilt the guitar as you play it.

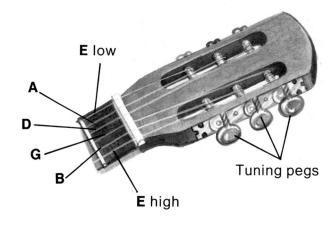

Strumming

The easiest way to play the guitar is to brush your right hand thumb across the strings. This is called strumming. Here is what you do: first, make sure you are sitting and holding your guitar correctly, without tilting it. Then rest your thumb against the **E** string (low) — the one nearest to you — and firmly brush your thumb over each of the strings in one downward movement. Practice playing like this until all six strings sound as if they are being played together.

Tuning your Guitar

You may need to ask an adult to help you to tune your guitar. To find the right notes you can use guitar pitch pipes, or play the notes on the piano. Tune each string on your guitar by turning the tuning pegs very gently, until the string sounds the same note as your pitch pipe or piano.

Pitch pipes

Chords and chord boxes

Two or more different notes sounding together make a chord, and you can accompany a song by strumming chords. The left-hand fingers make the notes of the chords by pressing down the strings at the correct places. Look at the chord boxes to find out which fingers to use and where to place them. A chord box is like the head of the guitar in miniature.

Left hand finger numbers

Strumming G

Place your right hand thumb against string **D** and firmly brush down over the remaining four strings. An X sign above a string on a chord box tells you not to strum that string. Practice your **G** chord by counting a steady four and strumming on each count. Now turn over to play and sing your first song!

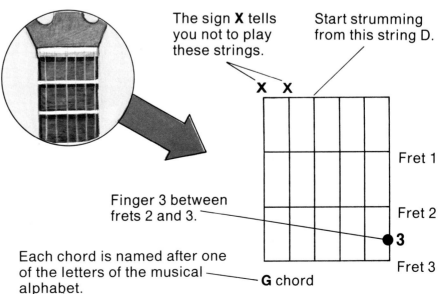

The sign **X** tells you not to play these strings.

Start strumming from this string D.

Finger 3 between frets 2 and 3.

Each chord is named after one of the letters of the musical alphabet.

G chord

Fret 1

Fret 2

3

Fret 3

Guitar Tunes

All the tunes on these pages can be sung or played on the recorder or piano, while you accompany on your guitar. Have fun!

Ten in the Bed

This song only uses the chord **G**.

Not too fast

G

There were TEN in the bed And the lit-tle one said, "Roll
NINE (etc.)

o – ver! Roll o – ver!" So they

all rolled o – ver and one fell out.

Last verse:
There was ONE in the bed,
And the little one said,
"Goodnight, Goodnight!"
Then slowly rolled over,
And fell asleep. . .

Two More Chords

Here are two more chords for you to learn. Practice strumming them, and then try changing from one chord to another. Now you are ready to play *Jingle Bells*.

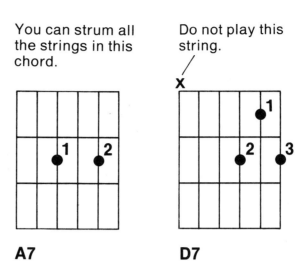

You can strum all the strings in this chord.

Do not play this string.

A7   D7

Jingle Bells

This song uses three chords, **G**, **D7**, and **A7**.

Lively

G

Jin – gle bells,   jin – gle bells,   Jin – gle all the way

D7   G   A7   D7

Oh, what fun it is to ride In a   one–horse o – pen sleigh.

G

Jin – gle bells,   jin – gle bells,   Jin – gle   all the way

D7   G   D7   G

Oh, what fun it is to ride In a   one–horse o – pen sleigh.

Making up your own Music

What kinds of sounds do your instruments make?

Swishing sounds . . .

tapping sounds . . .

bell-like sounds . . .

shaking sounds . . .

unusual sounds . . . or have you found some different sounds that your instruments will make?

Making up your own music

You can use your instruments to make up your own music. What kinds of sounds might you hear from the objects in the picture? Can you describe these sounds with your instruments? First ask yourself what kind of sound is needed, then find the instrument that will be able to play it best.

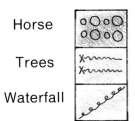

Horse		Train	
Trees		Bees	
Waterfall			

Writing your music down

You may want to write down your music to make your own "picture in sound." Try thinking of shapes, lines, or colors that will describe the sounds your instruments are making.

Recording your music

If you have a cassette recorder you could try making a recording of your "picture in sound." You could ask your friends to help you, and you could direct — like a conductor — telling your orchestra when to start and when to stop.

Music is Everywhere

Music is all around us. Sometimes you may not even realize that it is playing in the background. Sometimes you choose to listen to it. Different kinds of music have different effects:

Loud noisy music excites us . . .

at a film . . .

. . . or a concert maybe.

Gentle, quiet music helps us to relax . . .

when you go to see the dentist . . .

. . . or at home.

For many people music is their favorite hobby.

Writing a song . . .

playing in your own band . . .

learning to play an instrument . . .

listening to music at home . . .

singing in a choir . . .

going to a concert.

Index

Answers to page 17.
The violin and the double bass are members of the string section. The bass clarinet and bassoon are both wind instruments. The trombone is a brass instrument, and the cymbal, bass drum and gong are all percussion instruments. The harp is a stringed instrument, but it is always plucked with the fingers, and never played with a bow.

Acknowledgments

The publishers would like to thank the following for kindly
supplying photographs for this book:

Page 8 Travel Photo International (top), David Refern (center left), Travel Photo International (center right), BBC (bottom left), Jane Placca (bottom right), 9 CBS Records (top left), Clive Barda/Peter Thompson Associates (top right), ZEFA (center), David Redfern (bottom left), The Hutchison Library (bottom right); 16 Clive Barda; 17 Clive Barda; 30 David Redfern; 31 David Redfern.

Picture Research: Elaine Willis